Lectionary Stories *for* Preaching *and* Teaching

Lent and Easter Seasons Edition Cycle C

for the Revised Common Lectionary

A Compendium of Stories from
StoryShare
a Component of **SermonSuite.com**
from CSS Publishing Company

CSS Publishing Company, Inc.
Lima, Ohio

LECTIONARY STORIES FOR PREACHING AND TEACHING
LENT AND EASTER SEASONS EDITION, CYCLE C

FIRST EDITION
Copyright © 2013
by CSS Publishing Co., Inc.

Published by CSS Publishing Company, Inc., Lima, Ohio 45807. All rights reserved. No part of this publication may be reproduced in any manner whatsoever without the prior permission of the publisher, except in the case of brief quotations embodied in critical articles and reviews. Inquiries should be addressed to: CSS Publishing Company, Inc., Permissions Department, 5450 N. Dixie Highway, Lima, Ohio 45807.

For more information about CSS Publishing Company resources, visit our website at www.csspub.com, email us at csr@csspub.com or call (800) 241-4056.

ISBN-13: 978-0-7880-2717-8
ISBN-10: 0-7880-2717-4

PRINTED IN USA

Table of Contents

Introduction   5

Ash Wednesday   7
2 Corinthians 5:20b—6:10
Darkness Before the Light

Lent 1   12
Romans 10:8b-13
Aren't You Ashamed?

Lent 2   14
Genesis 15:1-12, 17-18
As Clear as the Milky Way

Lent 3   18
Isaiah 55:1-9
God's Dinner Bell

Lent 4   21
2 Corinthians 5:16-21
The Ugliest Man in the World

Lent 5   25
Psalm 126
Panic and Recovery

Passion / Palm Sunday   28
Luke 22:14—23:56
Passionate Sense

Maundy Thursday   32
1 Corinthians 11:23-26
Julia Gilbert Changes Love Feast Among the Brethren — Twice!

Good Friday   35
John 18:1—19:42
Betrayal in the Third Grade

Easter Day   39
Acts 10:34-43
Eyewitnesses

Easter 2   41
Acts 5:27-32
We Must Obey God

Easter 3   44
Acts 9:1-6 (7-20)
The Good Little Girl

Easter 4   48
John 10:22-30
Who Do You Trust?

Easter 5   50
Revelation 21:1-6
Everything Old Is New Again

Easter 6   52
John 14:23-29
The Great Starvation Experiment

Ascension of Our Lord   55
Ephesians 1:15-23
The Eyes of the Heart Enlightened

Easter 7   58
John 17:20-26
In All His Glory

About the Authors   61

Introduction

Since you are reading this, you probably preach on a regular basis. It is important to not only bring God's word to the members of your congregation but to help make the gospel of Christ engaging and thought-provoking.

Most people know that Jesus, the Master Storyteller, very often used stories and parables to make an important point to his listeners about God's kingdom. Following his example, we know that helping people to understand God's word through the telling of a story not only provides additional interest in a message, but also makes that same message easier to understand.

Over the years, CSS has published thousands of relevant, interesting, and inspiring anecdotes and stories to season a pastor's sermon. Not only has CSS produced numerous books to aid pastors in this important part of ministry but CSS also has a weekly online service called **StoryShare**, a component of **SermonSuite.com**, that was created to bring preachers the most timely and relevant illustrations possible. This edition of stories and anecdotes, gleaned from **StoryShare** for Cycle C, are written to dovetail with the readings from the Revised Common Lectionary and will serve you well as extended illustrations or in many cases, stand-alone sermons.

It is our hope that the stories in this book will not only assist you, the pastor, in your preaching but will also help you throughout your ministry.

The editors at CSS Publishing Company, Inc.

Ash Wednesday
2 Corinthians 5:20b—6:10
by Larry Winebrenner

Darkness Before the Light

Remember that thou art dust and unto dust thou shalt return.

Imposition of ashes reminds us of our mortality and immortality at once. Those very words used in the service when imposing ashes were used by the Lord to Adam when he sinned in the Garden of Eden.

But there's another reminder we should take to heart. Traditionally, the ashes come from the palms burned on the previous year's Palm Sunday. Christ marched victoriously into our lives. Although we executed him and laid him in the tomb "unto dust to return," Christ broke the bonds of sin we had tied him with, conquered death, and, through him, God revoked the sentence of death.

No wonder Paul cried, "We entreat you on behalf of Christ, be reconciled to God. For our sake he made him to be sin who knew no sin, so that in him we might become the righteousness of God" (2 Corinthians 5:20b-21).

Yet, the words should encourage us beyond this eternal reward. They should remind us that Christ accomplished this in the temporal world. We need not wait for eternity to have hope. God is at work in the world now.

Annie and Dowling Martin found this true in the darkest day of their lives back in 1928. When they married in 1899, Annie's father let the couple work a piece of land called variously Cavenders Branch or Cavenders Swamp. The couple farmed the land, built a barn, and lived in it while building a house.

They were dirt farmers in the poorest county in South Carolina but managed to enlarge the fields and raise nine children. Edna was the youngest girl, and she cared for Robert, three years younger than her, while the parents and other eight children worked the fields.

Like many six year olds, Edna was fascinated by fire. She especially loved the way those little sticks of wood with the red tip burst into flame when rubbed against a rough surface. And she found a whole box full of them! What fun to strike a match. Throw it down. Strike a match. Throw it down. Strike a match. Throw it down. The problem came when a loose piece of wallpaper caught fire. She didn't know what to do. She lugged Robert out into the yard and started screaming, "Mama! Mama!"

Dowling was in a far field plowing corn. The older boys were hoeing peanuts. The girls were picking beans, some to sell in town on Saturday, and some to can for the winter. Annie was in her flower garden. She sometimes made as much as a dollar on Saturdays selling flowers in Walterboro. But the flower garden was on the side of the house opposite to the side where the barn stood.

By the time Annie realized Edna was screaming for her, not playing at being mommy to Robert, Dowling had seen smoke rising from the house. He left horse and plow and raced across the furrows toward the house.

Frank, the eldest son, heard his sister's screams. When he looked over toward her, he saw flames through the open door. He ran toward the open door when Annie yelled, "Stop Frank!" He didn't want to stop. His only earthly possession was a banjo. He wanted to save it

"My banjo, Mama," he said.

"Banjos can be replaced," she said. "Sons can't."

By the time Dowling arrived, the family was standing in a group watching the flames shooting out the windows, licking the eaves. "Didn't nobody do nothin'?" he asked, despair in his voice.

Annie stood there, tears in her eyes. All their clothes. All their furniture. All their dishes and cookware. All their mementos collected over the years. All their Christmas decorations so carefully packed away. All their photographs. Even their family Bible. Everything. She turned to her husband. "Do nothin'? Dowling, what'd we do? Form a bucket brigade with two water buckets and a well? Ain't nothin' gonna stop them pine boards from burnin' once they start." She took her pruning shears and walked back to the flower garden.

That night the family slept in the barn.

"What are we going to do now?" asked Annie, knowing that Dowling didn't know any more than she did.

"We'll have to move to the city where I can find work." Doubt filled his voice.

"God will show us a way." Then Annie was very quiet.

Someone once said it's darkest just before the dawn.

No one could have coaxed the Martin family into believing that dawn was about to break. But with the house gone, it was almost impossible to raise nine kids. And Annie was pregnant again. Dowling had to find work of some kind. His brother Charley, living in Beaufort, told Dowling there was work for carpenter's helpers in Beaufort.

Dowling's first inclination had been to go to Charleston or Savannah to find work. But big cities were scary… unknown. Beaufort wasn't that much larger than Walterboro. Still, it had an adjacent marine base that helped the economy. And Dowling did know something about carpentry work. He built his own house and barn. He had helped neighbors build theirs, too.

So the Martins loaded the old farm wagon with tools, chickens, a sow, and kids. They tied the cow to the back of the wagon. Annie dug some of her favorite bushes up by the roots and wrapped the ball of soil in moistened burlap and loaded them on the wagon. They drove the wagon the 35 miles from Walterboro to Beaufort. On the way they passed a house sporting a sign: "Fire wood for sale."

"Pull over there, Dowling," said Annie. "Maybe that fella will let our animals get a drink at his horse trough." Her motive for stopping, however, was not for water. She had an idea. "Having any luck selling firewood?" she asked, like some old curious woman.

"Little. Why? Y' wanna buy some?"

"Maybe. After we get settled. Do town folk come out here to buy?"

"Some, but it's a ways. Mos'ly folks goin' by."

"S'pose a coupla my boys wanted to buy a whole load. Could they get a good price?" asked Annie.

The old man considered her for a few moments. Then he said, "Tell ya what I'll do. I'll give it to them free. A free cord of wood for every cord they cut and split for me."

"Deal!" said Annie. "They'll be back tomorrow. Come on, Dowling. Let's get on to Beaufort."

The next spring Annie spoke at the Women's Missionary meeting at her church. She told the women at the meeting, "God sure works in funny ways. I thought God was punishing us for something when Edna caught our house on fire. I thought my life was ended. We'd spent thirty years building up that farm so we could buy it from Daddy. But we were too successful. Daddy wasn't eager to sell it. Every time we'd start talking about it, he'd raise the price. I'd ask why and he'd say it was worth more. If I said we made it worth more, he'd say if we didn't like it to move. Now he wants us to buy it and move back. But we have our own forty acres on Ladies Island. Dowling bought it from a man he works for just six months after we moved to Beaufort.

"My point is this. My daddy had us in a crunch. We couldn't buy and we didn't see how we could move. Then God took that accident by Edna to show us we could move. If we hadn't moved, my boys wouldn't have that wood yard.

If we hadn't moved, we wouldn't have that farm on Ladies Island. If we hadn't moved, I wouldn't be here with you. It was Edna that struck the matches, but God that made us move."

Lent 1
Romans 10:8b-13
By C. David McKirachan

Aren't You Ashamed?

I remember when everybody was Presbyterian. I was a kid. The church was a city of people, everybody going to Sunday school, choir, fellowship happenings, and worship. My father, the pastor, was a public figure, welcomed into the parlors and the chambers of the decision makers.

It isn't so now. It is kind of passe to be a Christian, especially if you aren't in a church with stadium seating and on television. We're not part of the social or political elite. We're received with great reservation by anyone who is a reasonable, intelligent, intellectual. I mean, who the hell believes all this stuff? Why don't we just stick to a humanistic agenda and stop messing around with all the old superstitious stories? Aren't they just so much antique sloppy thinking? Haven't we proven that the soul doesn't exist and love is little more than an enzyme?

So for us to proclaim Jesus Christ is Lord is a rather embarrassing social *faux pas* rather than a courageous announcement of faith.

Well, sorry to embarrass any of you who are reasonable and philosophically centered in a universe that needs no God, but I'm a dumb and old-fashioned cousin who comes from the backwater of Calvinism. In my silly retrograde stubbornness, I continue to preach a gospel that is not based on metaphor, but on the actual incarnation of a loving and personal spirit that infuses and sanctifies the universe.

I regret if this causes you to hem and haw a bit. I mean, I do periodically have interesting insights and I don't fit the profile of a Bible-thumping evangelist. But it's where I happen to stand in life and such is the truth. I will remind you that there is room at the table, the communion table that is. There is room there even for secular humanists. How could that be? Well, I'm not sure. If there is room for Jews and Greeks in the family of God, there might be room there for a few of you. I know you'd be slumming it. But you might give it a try. It's a fascinating anthropological phenomenon how these intelligent, educated, experienced people continue to believe in this Christianity business.

It may not be the center of social acceptance anymore. But it's still the way, the truth, and the life.

Thank you for your kind indulgence. Have a nice day.

Lent 2
Genesis 15:1-12, 17-18
by Scott Dalgarno

As Clear as the Milky Way

> *After these things the word of the LORD came to Abram in a vision, "Do not be afraid, Abram, I am your shield; your reward shall be very great." But Abram said, "O Lord GOD, what will you give me, for I continue childless, and the heir of my house is my cousin, Eliezer of Damascus?"* — Genesis 15:1-2

Jay and Sarah found each other in college. Neither had dated much in high school. College represented a chance for both of them to get a new start and that was part of the bond that brought them together. They saw it in one another's eyes and in the geeky awkwardness each found attractive in the other.

They were engaged with astonishing speed, the way young people often are who find their first "true love." Their bond was strong. They felt as if they were meant for each other from before birth. Love was running away with them like a carriage without a driver. They decided they wanted four children. They even named them.

By their senior year, the "new" having worn off, both wondered if they had been emotionally hasty. Jay, in particular wondered what it would have been like had he tested the waters with several women before settling on one for life. They broke it off each assuring the other that they could always get back together if they wanted. The arrangement felt odd and reassuring at the same time.

Jay worked that summer at his father's restaurant in Seattle. He enjoyed his freedom but when September rolled around and, for the first time in his life, Jay found himself *not* going to school, he began to wonder if he had made a great mistake, breaking it off with Sarah. Taking the Labor Day weekend off, he made the three-hour drive hoping to surprise her, just showing up at her door.

He rang the bell with a giddy confidence but was a bit unnerved at her mother's initial unease at seeing him. Jay chalked it up to the breakup until she told him, haltingly, almost apologetically, that Sarah had been seeing someone else all summer and was once again, engaged.

Jay didn't have the heart to hang around another minute. He motored right home and did his best to move along in life. He applied to graduate schools all on the east coast thinking he needed a completely fresh start. Though he liked the fall colors in New England as much as anyone, he felt a certain culture shock, but when the next fall rolled around he dug into his studies and things went well enough for him to stick it out.

He more than welcomed the opportunity to go home for the holidays. It would be fun and his older brother was getting married right after Christmas. Jay would be a best man before he would be a groom. That felt somehow correct.

He found he thoroughly enjoyed planning a party for this brother. They had never been all that close before. On the big day Jay found himself listening very intently to everything the minister said during the ceremony. He saw himself right there, holding a woman's hands in his own.

He found the reception not to his taste, hating DJs and the obligatory playing of "Y-M-C-A" and "We Are Family," but he danced with a half dozen girls, asking Julie, his second cousin, to take several turns with him on the parquet floor. She seemed to enjoy the festive nature of it as much as he did. They managed to get together every day that vacation and, back at school, separated by 3,000 miles, they emailed often. Within weeks they found themselves talking about marriage, first, in general, then in reference to themselves.

It was odd, having a relationship develop that way, so far apart. There was something a bit unreal about it all, but Jay felt he wasn't getting any younger and he and Julie had quite a bit in common. With spring break coming, he bought her a ring and presented it to her at the family restaurant at an Easter morning brunch right in front of his family. Every one seemed so pleased for them both.

Later on that same morning he ran into his former fiancé Sarah's brother at church. He heard himself asking about Sarah. Was she well? Did she like being married? Dave, her brother, said that though she was still seeing Rick they hadn't married, and hadn't even set a date yet. Dave wrote down her number and presented it to Jay, encouraging him to call her. "She'd love hearing from you," he said.

Jay complied. He complied so quickly he called her from the narthex. He felt something break up inside himself at the word, "Hello." It was uncanny. It was like a spring thaw.

The two caught up quickly on the basics, but neither said anything to the other about their significant relationships. Then there was a long pause. How about coffee the next day, he said? Sarah related that she was leaving town to spend a week at the beach with her folks the next morning. She'd like to see him but it had to happen that afternoon. Jay said he had plans to do some shopping, but that it could probably wait a day, though he knew very well that he'd be on an airplane the next afternoon.

He thought about Sarah all the way through the service and was on his way to her house before the benediction was pronounced. Her mother answered the door once again, but this time she was chuckling.

Jay marveled at how easy it was catching up with Sarah. How it seemed they hadn't been apart a single day. They talked about everything — old friends, some of whom had already married and divorced. They talked about school, work, family, and pretty soon Sarah was crying and Jay found himself holding her in his arms. They talked the whole night.

It was near midnight when he finally asked her why she had gotten herself engaged again so quickly. "Oh," she said, "maybe it was because there wasn't a single thing about him that reminded me of you."

That night on the airplane, looking out at the stars, Jay felt shell-shocked. He was now promised to one woman and totally in love with another. He knew deep inside what he had to do. But what would he tell Julie? How would he break it to her?

Still, his heart was soaring now. His perspective was galactic. Why had he not seen this before? Any time he'd put himself in charge of engineering his own happiness, he'd made a mess of it. Life was so much bigger than he was, he thought. Everything of real worth was a gift, not contrived. It was as clear as the Milky Way.

Lent 3
Isaiah 55:1-9
by Rick McCracken-Bennett

God's Dinner Bell

Ho, everyone who thirsts, come to the waters; and you that have no money, come, buy and eat! Come, buy wine and milk without money and without price. Why do you spend your money for that which is not bread, and your labor for that which does not satisfy? Listen carefully to me, and eat what is good, and delight yourselves in rich food. — Isaiah 55:1-2

Growing up, I always thought we should have had a dinner bell. My friend Jim, who lived on another farm a mile or so away — less if you trekked through the woods, through the swamp (what we now more elegantly call a wetland), across his dad's fields, and up his lane to his house — *he* had a dinner bell. The bell was gold-colored, probably brass. There was a rope that hung from some sort of rocker deal on top of the bell. It was mounted on a post, right near the side door that led to the kitchen, and if you were in the kitchen, you could go out the door and walk a few steps to the summer kitchen, where it was a lot cooler to cook on those hot summer days.

In the summer we would play together almost every day. And just before noon, if it had already been cleared with my mother, the dinner bell would ring and we would race to the house to clean up and sit down to a real farmer's meal, complete with all the foods that most of us banned from our diets years ago. She didn't have to ring twice. She didn't have to say, "Stop your fooling around and get your fannies in here." She just had to give it a ring and we would take off running, brushing the dirt off of our jeans in puffs like smoke, salivating like a couple of Pavlov's dogs.

After a prayer, we would stuff ourselves and drink gallons of sweetened ice tea (which, for reasons that are lost in my childhood memory bank, we called "bug juice"). There was always enough food. Actually, there was always more than enough. If I brought my little brother along, there was enough. If we invited Steve up the road and Randy rode his bike over, there was enough. "Come and get it," the bell would say. "Eat up!" it rang. And we would eat and talk and laugh and tell stories. I remember feeling that I was just about the luckiest kid around, to have such good friends, and to have such wonderful food to eat.

We were always allowed to play in their barn. But one thing was off limits. It was a rope — a big, thick, rough rope that hung from one of the rafters and had a huge knot on the end. His folks would warn us to never, ever swing from that rope. It was too dangerous. But, of course, we did swing from it... every day we played together. One afternoon it was my turn to swing out of the hayloft and down to the floor. Apparently I grabbed the rope at a lower place than usual and like a modern-day bungee jumper who miscalculated the distance to the ground, I hit the floor and the momentum dragged me several more feet, pulling my shin over the head of a nail that was sticking out of the floor. I still have the scar. We were afraid to tell his mom, but what could we do? My jeans were ripped and bloodied. As expected, Jim's mother hit the roof — just like my mom would do later. Jim's mother cleaned up my wound, poured on something that both stung and stained, and after applying the bandage, sent us out to the porch to sit and not say a word while she called my mom to come and get me. I don't know if the wound or the scolding hurt more.

I didn't return to Jim's for a couple of days. It was probably my punishment. And when I was finally allowed to go over I thought that things would be different, that his parents wouldn't treat me the same, that there would be more and stricter rules. But as I climbed their front steps his mother greeted me with an ice-cold glass of sweetened bug juice. She said that she expected me to stay for dinner. And it was all like before, except that now I knew what it meant to have done something wrong, receive the punishment I deserved, and then be welcomed back to the banquet. And what a wonderful feeling it was!

Lent 4
2 Corinthians 5:16-21
by David O. Bales

The Ugliest Man in the World

All spring of 1939, Flora had tried to get her daughter Aida to attend Sunday school at the American church. But Paris was always more interesting. Aida, the only American in the *lycée*, seemed to be invited to every event on every weekend by every other student. Besides, after finally agreeing to attend Sunday school, Aida found that the teacher spoke English poorly. "I think Monsieur Sordet teaches the class so he can practice his English. I can hardly understand him. The three Brits in class just turn their heads and laugh. And really," Aida sniffed as she tapped her index finger on her mother's wrist, "Monsieur Sordet is the ugliest man in the world."

Besides trying to get Aida to Sunday school at the American church, Flora had all she could manage as a single mother and bread-winner. Her job at the U.S. embassy was already overwhelming. Embassy desks were stacked high with requests for visas from Spanish refugees. Flora would say, "America just isn't granting visas to Spaniards. But I'll phone the Mexican embassy and tell them I'm sending you over." Now, along with the Spaniards who'd escaped to France during the Spanish Civil War, refugees poured into Paris from Germany. The embassy staff called them "Hitler's flotsam and jetsam": German intellectuals and Jews. Many of them resembled Flora's grandparents. Some resembled Flora herself.

With the added stress of trying to save lives, Flora remained faithful to weekly worship and called upon her faith as she'd never considered possible. She prayed almost constantly during working hours as people waited in line to see her. They stood outside the embassy, lining up around the block. The same people returned every week, asking and then begging for a visa to America — and becoming thinner and more threadbare.

Flora and Aida's lives hung by the thinnest financial thread. Three years earlier Flora and Skip had received the telegram accepting his proposal for study at the Louvre. They didn't know and couldn't predict that his weak aortic artery would burst, leaving him dead in less than a minute and leaving Flora and Aida stranded in France without a job or support. Flora had struggled through grief and poverty at the same time, and she believed that her prayers were answered when she got the job at the embassy.

Aida's time was consumed by her high school chums. Flora's energy was daily sapped by inspecting outdated or obviously forged passports and saying, "I'm sorry. There're just no visas for the U.S."

Flora continued to pray until praying wasn't an act of will but of her nature. Only occasionally did Flora get Aida to Sunday school, and she'd come home with some complaint about Monsieur Sordet. "Mom, when he tries to read through those thick glasses, he looks like he's peering through a couple of portholes."

Their frayed existence began thoroughly to unravel when Hitler shattered the precarious phony war in May 1940. France formally surrendered on June 22. Although they were U.S. citizens, Flora's having Jewish grandparents placed them in instant jeopardy. She'd seen and heard enough from German refugees not to wait for Nazi troops to march into Paris.

Two days before the Germans occupied Paris, neighbors offered her and Aida a place in a car fleeing south. In twelve minutes they'd stuffed a suitcase apiece. In what was soon to become Vichy France, the port of Marseille beckoned as an open door out of a house fire.

On their second day, the car ran out of gas and no one would sell them more. Amid the scuffling and shoving of other refugees, they became separated from their neighbors when they entered a village. Within two kilometers beyond the village they were robbed of everything — including passports and visas.

Now only their physical strength could get them to safety. Flora and Aida walked every day. A few villagers gave them a little to eat. More often, low on food for themselves and low on patience with strangers, they warned refugees to keep moving.

Two weeks later and fifteen pounds lighter they arrived in Marseille and learned that two groups were helping refugees. They leaped at the hope. As they walked into the small hotel room to meet the Assistance Committee, a voice in broken English greeted them: "Ah, Aida. I'm so glad to see you." Hugs and tears followed between Aida, Flora, and Monsieur Sordet.

After a week's hiding and preparing, they were instructed to arrive at exactly 6 a.m. at a particular ship on the waterfront. Monsieur Sordet rushed up to them. He handed them passports and visas and hustled them onto the ship. The gangplank pulled up behind them and the ship immediately began to move. They had a moment to wave to Monsieur Sordet. He looked up at them through his giant glasses and waved back, then walked away quickly. They were on their way to the Caribbean island of Martinique and from there to the United States.

Flora and Aida stood with an arm around each other, watching their beloved France recede. For the first time in weeks they both breathed normally. Flora was still praying. She said to Aida, "Now what do you think of Monsieur Sordet?"

Aida tugged a little on her mother, rocking her slightly. She said, "I think he's about the handsomest man in the world."

Lent 5
Psalm 126
by Sandra Herrmann

Panic and Recovery

Many of us have experienced the total panic that ensues when we discover that our wallet has been lost — or, God forbid, stolen. We frantically search our various pockets or purses. We check the bedroom — maybe when I undressed yesterday I dropped it? Maybe it fell off the dresser or table? Well, before moving furniture I'll go out and look in the car. It would be easy enough for it to fall out as I got into the car or out of it.

Once out at the car, we have to check under the seats. If your wallet is thinner than mine, you'll run your hand between the seat and the back. Check the backseat too, because if it fell out in the car it could have slid through to the backseat. Be sure to run your hand as far under as you can reach.

Well, this is distressing. If it's not in the car and it wasn't where it should have been in the house, where could it be? Now it's time to sit down, breathe a little, and think. Where do you last remember seeing it?

The last time I had this experience, I had been at church. I remembered taking it out of my pocket/purse to pay for supper. At the time I was concerned because I thought I had taken the money I got at the ATM and put it in my wallet, but the cash wasn't there. I had to write a check. I checked my purse again and found the checkbook still in my purse.

I had stopped to get gas after that. Did I have my wallet then? I realized that I wasn't sure if I had the wallet, because I had discovered the ATM money in my coat pocket. But I hadn't reached for my wallet at the time — I just paid with cash.

Oh dear. Well, time to call the gas station. Was my wallet turned in? No? Are you *sure*? Okay, thanks.

Called church. Was a wallet like mine turned in to the secretary? Did the pastor see it by chance? No. But the secretary will pray for me to find it. That's nice of her. Maybe that will even work.

I went back to the bedroom and tracked my movements of the night before as best I could. Oh Lord, help me find that wallet. One good thing: I know there wasn't cash in it. Just my credit cards, driver's license, blood bank card, two gift cards I haven't used yet, insurance cards, my ID for the Y, my MedicAlert© card with half my life's information, my ATM card. (Oh, I'd better check my pockets! Do I remember putting it back in my wallet or is it with the cash in my pocket?) It's in the wallet. Well, at least no one can get my money without the PIN.

The more I think about how bad this whole thing is, the less sure I am of anything. And I'm starting to worry about contacting all those companies to get my cards stopped, just in case it was stolen. I'm starting to pace, worrying, looking in places I've already looked just in case.

So I hopped in the car and drove only slightly above the speed limit to get to the church so I could search there. It's not in the coat area. Not under the couch where I'd sat and talked with a friend. If it had been under any of the tables or chairs, someone would have taken it to the secretary's office, or even called me, because I had accurate identification in there.

Then I realize — I went into the sound room to talk to the techs about getting a CD of the Sunday service. I'd sat down for a minute while they got out the CD and put it in a case. Could the wallet be in there? Last chance. If it's not here, it's really gone, and maybe stolen. From the church, of all places. But when I bent over and looked, there it was, hiding under a chair in the sound room. Whew!

I went back to the secretary's office and said, "Rejoice with me, for the lost is found!" And she did. I laughed, and we talked about the panic that ensues when you can't find your wallet or your keys. I'm babbling about this event. I realize that I'm positively giddy.

Since I've never been a refugee, never been torn from my home and family and carried away to a foreign land against my will, I will never know how those returning from Babylon felt. But in the words of this Psalm and my words: "You restored my fortune, O Lord, and I, who was terrified, have reaped with a song of joy. Thank you, God, for helping me find my life again."

I sang hymns of praise all the way back home.

Passion / Palm Sunday
Luke 22:14—23:56
by Peter Andrew Smith

Passionate Sense

Suzanne began straightening hymnbooks and picking up leftover bulletins as soon people started leaving the church. Somehow worship didn't seem complete for her unless everything was ready for the next service. After a few minutes, the only one left in the church was a young man sitting in the back with his head bowed.

"Sorry," he said as she worked her way over to him. "I guess I should be leaving."

Suzanne motioned for him to remain. "You stay as long as you like. No one should ever be rushed out of church."

"Thanks," he said with a slight smile, and he bowed his head again.

She continued her trek through the pews but snuck an occasional glance his way. She thought the young man looked familiar, but she couldn't remember if he usually came by himself or with someone else.

Suzanne reached the final pew and deposited the collected papers in the recycling bin. She made sure the other doors were locked and went back into the sanctuary. The young man was still deep in thought. She quietly walked down the side aisle and slipped into the seat beside him.

He saw her and smiled again. "I suppose you need me to go so you can lock up."

"I'm not in a hurry to go anywhere," she said, extending her hand. "I've seen you here before, but I can't put a name to you. My name is Suzanne."

"Chuck," he said, shaking her hand. "I work at the hospital in the labs."

"Pleased to meet you," she said. "You still thinking about this morning's service?"

"I am. Hearing the story of Jesus all the way from the Last Supper to the cross is pretty intense."

"It sure is," Suzanne said. "Every time I hear it I discover something new."

"Really?"

"Sure. This morning I was struck by how no one knew what to do with Jesus. After he was arrested they kept sending him here and there before Pilate finally condemned him. They seemed confused as to what to do with him."

"Huh," Chuck said. "I can understand that, because I'm not sure what to do with Jesus either."

"What do you mean?"

"Well," he said, "there seems to be so much in the story — his breaking bread with the disciples, his time in the garden, his trial, and his death on the cross. I'm not sure what all of it means." He looked into her face. "Why did Jesus die?"

"That's a good question, and I think the pastor could probably answer that one better than me," Suzanne said. "But I know it's because Jesus loves us and wanted to save us from sin and death."

"I've heard that explanation before, but I can't understand it up here," he said, pointing to his head.

"Hmm, I'm not sure that love ever makes sense up there." Suzanne rubbed her chin for a moment. "You got a wife or a girlfriend?"

"Yeah."

"You understand in your head why she loves you?"

"No," Chuck said with a smile. "Sometimes for the life of me I don't know why she does."

"But when she does something loving," Suzanne said, pointing to his chest, "you know it in there, don't you?"

"I sure do."

"I think that's why they call those parts of the gospel the Passion. We're meant to feel them in our hearts even when we can't sort them out in our heads."

"But how can I feel it in my heart?" he asked.

"Well, I use this time of year to walk with Jesus through the story."

"But it's Jesus' story, not mine."

Suzanne shook her head. "No, Chuck. I know that Jesus means the story to be ours too because he kept people with him the whole way — and asks us to be there too."

"What do you mean?"

"Who was in the upper room?"

"The disciples," Chuck answered, "but wasn't Jesus alone in the garden when he prayed?"

"Naw, there were disciples with him, although they kept falling asleep. And they were there when he got arrested."

"Ah, Suzanne, but then they all ran away."

"Yeah, most of them might have, but remember that Peter followed. And I bet some of those fellows around when Jesus went on trial were followers, even if they didn't dare say it."

"But Jesus was alone after he was condemned."

"No, there were disciples around him then as well. They may have been at a distance and horrified by what they saw, but they were there to watch Jesus die."

Chuck thought about it for a while. "So you think that by hearing those stories and thinking about being there I'll understand them?"

"I'm not sure," Suzanne said, "but you'll experience them, and I think that is why the gospel writers wrote them for us."

Chuck looked at her for a few minutes and took her hand. "Thank you."

"Always a pleasure," Suzanne said. "And don't forget that the Passion isn't the only thing to experience this time of year."

Chuck tilted his head to one side. "What do you mean?"

"The journey to the cross isn't finished until we reach Easter morning," Suzanne said. "See you next Sunday?"

"I'll be here," Chuck said.

Suzanne followed him out the door as she knew that everything was finally ready for the next time of worship.

Maundy Thursday
1 Corinthians 11:23-26
by Frank Ramirez

Julia Gilbert Changes Love Feast Among the Brethren — Twice!

For I received from the Lord what I also handed on to you...
— 1 Corinthians 11:23a

The venerable elders of the old Dunkers, one of the German Plain People sometimes referred to as the Pennsylvania Dutch, would meet yearly to argue their arcane understanding of the scriptures in order to be true in their faith and practice. What they received from their reading of the Lord's word they assiduously handed on to the next generation. They changed, if at all, very slowly. Though in theory anyone could speak at their Annual Meetings, in practice the respect accorded to their elders, with their long beards and plain garb, meant that they had a greater voice.

Nowhere were traditions more honored than in the long and complex ritual known as the Love Feast. This communion service, often stretching over three days, included a foot-washing ceremony and an agape meal, along with the bread and cup. This was their signature practice, which others found so intriguing that many would come to witness the celebration.

So it is all the more surprising that these traditions were changed — twice — by a woman who was disabled, once when she was a teenager, and once decades later after a lifelong struggle.

Julia Gilbert (1844-1934) was born near the foot of South Mountain in Frederick County, Maryland, but when she was four her family moved to Wolfe Creek in western Ohio. She attended her first Annual Meeting at the age of six and rarely missed another through her long life.

When she was eight years old, two of her siblings died when they contracted measles and scarlet fever. She barely survived herself and was crippled for life.

In 1858, at the age of fourteen, she was baptized in the rushing stream. At first she was reluctant to step into the water in her fragile condition, afraid of being swept away, but her pastor reminded her that Jesus had been there before. Recalling the baptism of Jesus by John the Baptist, she stepped out into the river and as she knelt she prayed, "Dear God, I promise to you that I will live faithful to Jesus until I die." She kept that promise.

She eagerly looked forward to the Love Feast that was celebrated following her baptism as a meal she was sharing with Jesus. The experience was joyful but that night she found she could not sleep, and she finally lit a candle and read John 13:4: "He riseth from supper, and laid aside his garments; and took a towel, and girded himself."

The next day she asked her father why the Wolfe Creek congregation had performed the foot washing and then set the meal on the table. Shouldn't they have set the meal on the table and then, like Jesus, risen from the table for the foot washing? Her father, according to her report, sighed and answered, "The old Brethren took the ordinance from several passages of scripture and thought this to be the proper way it ought to be done." This satisfied her for a day or two but eventually she questioned the elders, and the next year the congregation changed the way they performed Love Feast to conform to the fourteen-year-old's reading of scripture.

By contrast, her next cause took nearly fifty years before it was successfully concluded. In her day, men passed a long strip of communion bread to each other, each breaking off a piece, but the women did not break bread with each other. Instead, an elder walked down the row and the sisters broke off a piece. This did not seem biblical to Julia, nor was she satisfied with the official explanations for the practice. For decades, first in Ohio and later in Iowa, where she moved after her parents' deaths, she championed the cause, only to see it tabled or returned at Annual Meetings. Finally in June of 1910, at Winona Lake, Indiana, Julia herself spoke on the floor of Annual Meeting, saying, "When I was baptized, I made a vow to God to walk in all his ways and to read the scriptures. I believe it is our duty to do things the way Jesus taught us to do them." The motion passed and the next year the sisters broke the bread among themselves.

Paul wrote his exhortation to the Corinthians not to preserve some imagined purity of practice — what he had passed on was the practice of coming together at the table to commemorate the Passion of Jesus Christ. A reading of the larger context of the text makes it clear that the real problem in Corinth was that not all were sharing equally around the table. Rich were arriving early and eating all the good food of the agape meal, leaving the poor, who worked, to eat later and less. Regardless of the century in which we live, Jesus calls us as equals to his table, prepared to listen and learn from each other, and to recognize that the Spirit dwells richly among us all.

Good Friday
John 18:1—19:42
by Rick McCracken-Bennett

Betrayal in the Third Grade

> *So Judas brought a detachment of soldiers together with police from the chief priests and the Pharisees, and they came there with lanterns and torches and weapons. Then Jesus, knowing all that was to happen to him, came forward and asked them, "Whom are you looking for?" They answered, "Jesus of Nazareth." Jesus replied, "I am he." Judas, who betrayed him, was standing with them.* — John 18:3-5

> *One of the slaves of the high priest, a relative of the man whose ear Peter had cut off, asked, "Did I not see you in the garden with him?" Again Peter denied it, and at that moment the cock crowed.* — John 18:26-27

(Kids say the darnedest things... sometimes, like adults, they say the most awful things.)

You would be inclined to give them a break. After all, they were only third-grade boys.

You would say, "They were too young to have known what they were doing," or "Knowing right from wrong, especially in this case, would be too difficult for nine- and ten-year-old boys to comprehend." And you would be right, and... you would be wrong.

It was fall; a new school year had just barely gotten underway. Even for the Midwest, it was warm, too warm to sit in a stuffy, old classroom with freshly varnished floors that reflected the room in swirly, uneven patterns. Recess, as always, was a welcome relief. This particular day they were going to get a little extra time on the playground. There was to be a softball game and everyone was invited to join in. All morning long the room was buzzing with third-grade wonderings about who among them co-captains Don and Randy, the best players in the whole elementary school, would pick for their team.

Recess didn't start when the first bell rang. The students stared at their teacher and then at each other, and she just sat sadly at her desk. Every minute or so she would pull open her middle desk drawer and rummage around a little before closing it and looking out at her class. Something was up and none of the kids knew what it was. They just sat there casting sideways glances at each other.

Finally Mrs. Watkins stood up, slid her chair in, cleared her throat, looked the class over, and spoke slowly and carefully. "I'm not sure how to say this, boys and girls. Someone has been in my desk and has stolen the milk money for this afternoon's snack." She paused, quickly swiped an eye with her fingers, and went on. "This is serious, because it means that one of us cannot be trusted. Someone here is a thief. And I suspect that some of you know who did this. So… we will not go out to recess, and we will not have our softball game; in fact, we will not have any recess until the person who took this money comes forward. I am so disappointed, boys and girls. I hope we can take care of this quickly."

The room went into shock. Not so much that the money had been stolen — few of the kids hadn't made off with a little change from their mother's purse from time to time — but rather because the softball game of the century and their chance to whip the fourth graders was being canceled. Stunned, the children sat there, and when Mrs. Watkins wasn't looking, snuck a glance with raised eyebrows and got shrugs from each other which said, "I don't know what to do either."

The second bell for recess rang out in the hallway.

An eternity passed when a crumpled-up note landed on Steve Richards' desk. Slowly, with his eyes steadily on his teacher, he unfolded the note. His eyes grew wide as he read, "Let's tell her that Robbie did it." Robbie wasn't a friend. In fact, few kids in the class liked him at all. Steve shot a glance at Randy, who nodded almost imperceptibly back at him, and then at Don — and there you had it, three third-grade co-conspirators. A couple more notes passed and they were ready with their plan.

As the third bell rang, telling the older kids to line up for recess, they stood, and with a nod to each other, Steve, Randy, and Don approached their teacher. Their guilty looks probably made Mrs. Watkins think that they were the guilty party. "Mrs. Watkins?" Randy took the lead. "Mrs. Watkins, we know who took the money."

"Yes?" she replied, looking dead into his eyes but with her face cocked to one side. "Who, then? Who did this?"

Randy looked at Steve and then at Don and then blurted out in a stage whisper, "Robbie... Robbie did it. Now, can we go to recess?"

"Go back to your seats," Mrs. Watkins said softly. "Everyone... may I have your attention?" Which wasn't necessary since everyone's eyes were fixed at first on the boys, and now on her. "I want you to line up for recess. Robbie... I would like you to remain here with me."

The class lined up and then made their way to the playground. But there was no softball that day. Randy and Don didn't pick teams. They and Steve Richards just stood together, unable to look each other in the eye. When the bell rang for them to return, they walked silently to the luke-warm drinking fountain and then to their classroom. Everyone sat down.

"Class? Robbie will not be with us for the next two days. He has been suspended for taking the milk money from my desk. When he returns I expect you to treat him in the same way that you would like to be treated if the shoe were on the other foot. Do you all understand?" The class nodded as one.

On the bus that afternoon, Randy and Steve and Don sat together in the back. "Now what are we going to do? What should we do? Should we tell Mrs. Watkins?" But the question that they couldn't quite answer, because after all they were just third-grade boys, was why he accepted his punishment when he was innocent? Why didn't he speak up? Why didn't he tell on them, for it was obvious who lied about him? And even though they didn't understand the deeper questions at the time, they thought often as they grew up about the sacrifice Robbie made that hot fall day.

It may be just a coincidence — yeah, that's probably it, just a coincidence — that Robbie became a minister out of college and is still to this day.

Easter Day
Acts 10:34-43
by Stan Purdum

Eyewitnesses

> ...*but God raised him on the third day and allowed him to appear, not to all the people but to us who were chosen by God as witnesses...* — Acts 10:40-41a

"It couldn't have been him," the distraught woman said. "I talked to him not more than an hour ago."

The police officer shifted uneasily on his feet. These things were never easy. "I'm so sorry, ma'am," he said, "but we identified him from his driver's license. And the car was registered in his name as well."

"Well, it's got to be a mistake. It's not him."

"Actually," replied the officer, "we will need someone to formally identify him."

"I'll do it." That was from the woman's sixteen-year-old son, Ryan. She didn't know how long he had been standing behind her but suddenly she was glad he was there. He was such a level-headed boy. He'd be able to straighten out this colossal mistake. One look and he'd know the man lying in morgue was not his father. And then the police could put their energies into finding out who the unfortunate driver was.

"Thank you, Ryan," she said. Then, turning to the officer, she added, "My son will go with you, and you'll see. It's not my Tom you've got there." The starch in her voice was almost convincing but both the officer and Ryan noticed the quiver in her lip.

"Is there someone we can call for you first?" the officer asked.

"Not necessary," the woman said, gathering her courage. "You'll have Ryan back in no time. You'll see."

It was less than an hour later when Ryan came back. But as he opened the door, his mother took one look at him and knew the awful truth.

They crumpled into each other's arms, sobbing with great grief.

* * *

"It couldn't have been him," Philip said. "They crucified him. All Jerusalem saw it. Nobody could have survived that. He's dead. I didn't want to believe it, but it's true."

Mary Magdalene could hardly stand still, even though she'd run all the way from the tomb. "But it was him," she said, "He spoke to me."

"You've got to be mistaken, woman. It's not him."

"Actually," replied Mary, "John and Peter have been to the tomb. It's empty."

"Yes, they told me. But all that proves is that his body has been moved."

Mary realized that Philip was not going to be convinced by anything she said, so finally she simply told him, "You just wait. You'll see."

Much later that day, she entered the house where the Eleven had been staying. Except for Thomas, they were all there.

And all ten of them were sobbing with great joy.

Easter 2
Acts 5:27-32
by John S. Smylie

We Must Obey God

We must obey God rather than any human authority.
— Acts 5:29b

He was only nineteen years old, more than a little idealistic and was about to engage in a spiritual journey that would last for a lifetime. After partying deep into the late hours of the night he resented the loud alarm clock demanding his attention, screaming out to him that it was time to get up, time to get out of bed and go to his sociology class. He had no idea that this day would be a day that would influence the rest of his life. After throwing water on his face and brushing his teeth, hoping to camouflage the scent of the previous night, he descended on the elevator from the top floor of his high-rise dorm room and faced the chilly air — and the steps that seem to be designed for dogs rather than human beings... annoying steps, one step up then another step to reach the next step up, thereby always having to use the same leg for the up step.

He reached his sociology class that met at the University Chapel, a space that could accommodate the over 800 students that gathered twice a week. This was a lousy learning environment, made even worse by a lack of sleep and a professor whose lecture might as well have been read from the assigned textbook. After class he walked down the dog steps and into the foyer of the dormitory, pushed the up button for the elevator, stepped inside, pushed 20, and ascended to the top floor. Throwing his books on his desk, he pulled the curtains shut and climbed back into bed. He fell asleep within a few minutes and had a dream that changed his life.

The dream was simple... he was given an image of himself as God saw him — an image that was very different than the one he had formed of himself. The dream offered him a vision of his life first as a young man, then as an old man. He was dressed in light, able to give and receive love, and he knew that he was glimpsing his truest self. Upon awakening he discovered that his mind had been branded by the powerful image that he knew was impressed upon him by God almighty. From that moment on he began to seek God's light.

When our lives are touched by the reality of the holy, we continue to have choices — yet our choices become narrower and at times more obvious. It seems that our choices are really quite simple: we either choose to obey God or we are miserable. The young man in this story would soon discover that he had to make a choice whether to follow the prompting of the Holy Spirit or to follow the wishes of his parents. He announced to his parents that he was leaving college to pursue a spiritual journey. His parents thought he was crazy and expressed their concerns in no uncertain terms; they didn't understand or support his decision to leave college. He needed to discover more about the power of God, while his parents understood that he needed an education to be successful in the world. But the Spirit was calling him to a different knowledge: "We must obey God rather than any human authority." He left college, returning later to complete his education after experiencing a journey that taught him about faith and holiness. That journey is another story too long to tell here.

Years later he found himself at a divinity school, preparing to serve as a minister, when the Spirit again called him to leave the seminary environment and also to sell everything that he had and give it to the poor. This time his mother nearly had a heart attack at the thought of him giving away the inheritance that he had received from her father, his grandfather. "We must obey God rather than any human authority."

He did leave the seminary, and he did sell everything he had and gave it to the poor — and to his surprise he was invited to live in a monastic community where he experienced daily worship, contemplative prayer, and the deep healing power of our Lord Jesus Christ. His journey continues to this day. As he listens for the wind of the Spirit and the call of Jesus, he continues to find himself in unexpected adventures with the choice of obedience to God always before him.

As we look at our lives, we may ask: What risk is the Spirit calling us to take? As we think of what God is doing in our faith communities, in our families, and in our personal lives, it may be good for us to ask ourselves if our faith communities, our families, and our personal lives show obedience to God rather than to human authorities, or even worse, to self-centered and sinful desires. A true journey of faith will likely take us to places that we never dreamed we would go, and yet we can be sure that we will be blessed and God will be honored if we choose to obey our Lord's will and live out his vision for each of us.

We can imagine those first apostles filled with the Spirit of God, filled with confidence and courage, filled with the desire to share the good news of the life-giving power over sin and death that they found in connecting their lives with the living God through the person of Jesus Christ. May our choices reflect the same obedience to God and may our lives show forth his presence in our communities, in our families, and in ourselves. Let us obey God rather than any human authority!

Easter 3
Acts 9:1-6 (7-20)
by Scott Dalgarno

The Good Little Girl

Kathleen had always been the good little girl and it had nearly killed her. As a child she found that whatever she did to please her mother, it usually made her father mad. And it went the other way too. She was an only child and her father wanted a son, so he did his utmost to make her into what pleased him. He took her shooting with him. He made her play baseball. She was no athlete, but she did her best — and her best at baseball and target practice always left her mother cold. When her mother would dress her in gingham, her father looked as if she were a total disappointment. Poor Kathleen didn't know what to do. But instead of complaining she did her best to comply with everyone. And it nearly made her sick.

Her frustration at the impossible task of pleasing everyone wasn't enough to sink her. No, she managed to marry (twice, in fact), have three children, finish her M.B.A., and take care of the everyday operations of a medium-sized bank for years. And every day she ran a gauntlet at home and work — because there is no way anyone on this planet can keep everybody within shouting distance smiling.

Still, she tried. There was the divorce and a remarriage, and still she set her sights on being the most compliant, most attractive, most nurturing wife and mother in the world. At work she put in sixty hours a week trying to keep everyone above and below her in a state of peace and productivity. She was good at it.

She had been a person of faith since childhood. Her mother's mother had seen to that, much to the chagrin of her father who wanted his daughter to be completely self-reliant, like he was. "What Would Jesus Do?" was her motto; she thought of her home and office as her ministry and viewed everyone around her as disciples who she felt she needed to keep clean and fed and on track.

"Give me strength, God" was her prayer every day — and God seemed to give it to her every morning... until she was about forty. That's when the wheels started to come loose from the great enterprise of her life.

The bank, locally owned for the first ten years she worked at it, had been bought by a large conglomerate. New policy statements were sent to her by the dozen. Every day there were fresh complaints from the troops and who did they come to? Kathleen, of course. She handled them as well as she could to begin with but in a matter of months her resolve began to crumble. She'd wake at two in the morning night after night trying to find a way through the mess. But she felt like the Dutch boy who put his fingers in the dike — new holes kept springing up.

When her husband Rick began complaining that things at home were not as they'd been and their two children, Becca and Brandi, began acting out all over the place, Kathleen knew a reckoning was coming.

Still, she forged ahead with superglue and duct tape until the Easter afternoon of her 41st year. The neighborhood was always invited to Kathleen and Rick's for brunch after church on Easter. And in they came — a score of them, with kids in tow. The smell of ham filled the house but there had been a glitch. Kathleen's famous twice-baked potatoes were a total loss — something about the sour cream being "off." Maybe it was that alone or maybe it was the fight she'd had with Rick that morning before church about him playing golf instead of helping with setting up, or the fact that Becca's retainer was lost for the hundredth time — whatever, Kathleen, for the first time in her life, melted down.

She'd lost her temper before, of course. But this time there was a definite break going on. She walked right past Mary Patterson, ignoring completely her apology for bringing her cousin Ginny without calling ahead. With the house full she retreated upstairs to her office and sat herself down in her late grandmother's overstuffed chair, where she began to let herself come unglued.

A size seven, she suddenly felt heavy, pressed down by the weight of what she felt was an entire life of failure. She felt a failure as a mother, a failure as a wife twice, a failure as a manager, a homemaker, a daughter. Suddenly all the things she had ever accomplished meant nothing to her and all the things she had wanted to do were like so much trash.

Right there, on that Easter afternoon with a houseful of guests, Kathleen unloaded completely on God. She told God that she had done her best to be a good mother and wife, a fine employee, a caring daughter and aunt and neighbor — and it all amounted to nothing. She was tired of trying. More than that, she was done with it. She no longer cared if the neighbors felt welcome in her home, no longer cared if her daughter's teeth were straight. It meant nothing to her that her husband loved her or that her son would pass the A.P. class she had tutored him in. She didn't care if her mother ever called, or if her boss praised her or fired her. She was exhausted in a way she had never known, and she was not at all interested in pleasing another human being for the rest of her life.

What surprised her was that she didn't feel the least bit guilty for her feelings, nor did she feel glad. In fact, she realized that she didn't feel anything at all. There, with the April sun streaming in on her from the skylight, she heard a line from Saint Therese uttered in her grandmother's voice — something she'd heard a hundred times but not for a dozen years — "If you can serenely bear the trial of being displeasing to yourself, you will be for Jesus a pleasant place of shelter."

Now, for the first time in her life, she took these words to heart. She knew that they were absolutely true and true for her. And in the stillness of that moment with the murmur of Easter company below her, she began to breathe deeply and easily, and she also began to heal.

Easter 4
John 10:22-30
by C. David McKirachan

Who Do You Trust?

Jesus wasn't a shepherd... and neither am I — but I'm pretty clear on this business of people who aren't part of the bunch not getting it. It's difficult at best to communicate the firm realities of salvation and hope to people who live in the darkness of a universe built on the hard realities of power and privilege, or measurable and attainable, or practical and profitable, or America and family, or any of the other normalities of our culture's mythological structure. "Tell us clearly whether or not you are the Christ." Such a demand is so weird that it boggles the mind. What did he need to do? What did they want? What proof would create the gravity that could break the hold of their expectation and judgment?

When I was ten, my older sister and I journeyed with my parents to the country estate of Miss Anne, one of the pillars of my father's church. "Rose Garden" (as it was known) was a working farm, animals and all. We were gussied up, so we had to be careful where we stepped and what we did. A pasture stretched out from a gate with stone posts. Out under trees on its far side, a small flock of sheep grazed. I was fascinated with them, and so my indulgent sister helped me over the gate and watched me journey toward the sheep, a bunch of green grass clutched in my hand as a peace offering and an incentive for them to trust me.

They bunched together, one of them (larger than the rest) making noises that sounded anxious. I kept on. Finally the big guy came toward me. I was encouraged and held out the offering. I remember wondering what one should say to a sheep. "Nice sheep" seemed lame, so I kept my silence and let the grass do the talking.

To make a long story short, the ram (which I'm sure he was) came close, reared up on his hind legs, and butted me in the middle. The only reason I didn't fall in the mud was because he stepped on my foot and I grabbed his head. At that point I took off running, with him in hot pursuit. My sister had climbed over the fence, laughing so hard she couldn't speak. So much for gentle sheep.

The basic problem was that I wasn't on the ram's list — I was a stranger. It wouldn't have mattered if I had some sheep candy and a bribe for the big guy. It wouldn't have mattered if I knew what to say. He was having none of it and none of me.

So maybe what they thought of Jesus' teaching and what they subsequently did to him is understandable. But *we aren't sheep!* We have choices to make that can bring us to new worlds of hope and abundant life. You'd think we'd learn. Maybe we're not hungry enough. Like those fat woolies on Miss Anne's farm, we're too well fed. We're not desperate enough to listen to a new voice. We want more proof. Oh well, missed the Lord again.

I wonder what was going through the ram's head when he chased me across the pasture. I wonder if he thought he won. My sister never told anybody about that day. She's cool.

Easter 5
Revelation 21:1-6
by Rick McCracken-Bennett

Everything Old Is New Again

See, I am making all things new.
— Revelation 21:5a

In Revelation (and other places in scripture) we're told that God is in the business of making all things new. What does that mean when the thing God is making new is us?

Years ago my baby sister wandered into a store — a junk store, really. She walked up and down the cluttered aisles not looking for anything in particular. She was just about ready to leave when a piece caught her eye. It was a bookstand — dusty, dirty, covered with (she found out soon enough) five layers of paint over the original varnish. "How much do you want for this?" was answered with "How much would you give?" and a few minutes and a little good-natured haggling later Kay walked out with her purchase.

She wasn't immediately struck with buyer's remorse; it was more like buyer's confusion. What was she going to do with it? How could she restore it? She had no idea.

Kay asked around at work and finally contacted a furniture refinisher. He gave her some ideas about what kind of noxious chemicals would remove the layers of paint. He told her a little about sanding and refinishing, and then he said, "But the most important thing is love. You've got to love the piece… see beyond the scratches and the paint and the dirt. You need to spend time with it, love it, and see it as it can be, not as it is."

So Kay spent time with it: holding it, looking at it, examining it from every angle until she got an idea about how the piece would look when it was finally restored. Then lovingly, carefully, she began to painstakingly strip off layer after layer of paint. When she reached bare wood she found that the gobs of paint had protected it so well that it didn't require much sanding at all. And when she was finished she gave this piece that she loved so much, that she made new, to me as a gift for my ordination. And most Sundays I use that stand on the altar at my church.

It seems to me that this is a lot like how God makes us new. The most important ingredient is God's love. It is God's love that sees past the layers and layers of junk and filth that I've wrapped around myself: my public image I have so carefully held on to; my habits and compulsions I rationalize away; my sin and my sins; my prejudices and hate.

And slowly, over time, God works God's love on me: peeling off a little here and a little there, and all the time knowing full well what is under all that crud. God looks at me with eyes of love and sees me as I really am, as I was created to be — and then, if I am willing, God begins to chip away and strip away what doesn't belong.

Unlike my treasured bookstand, the process with us takes a little longer — perhaps an entire lifetime. God no more strips away something than we find a substitute to fill the spot. Yet the longer God works on us and with us, the better we are able to see what God sees, and love what God loves, and begin to cooperate with the master refinisher to make all things new.

Easter 6
John 14:23-29
by Frank Ramirez

The Great Starvation Experiment

(Jesus said), "Peace I give, not as the world gives..."
— John 14:23-29

About midway between VE Day (May 8) and VJ Day (August 14) in the summer of 1945, *Life* magazine published an issue that included photographs of a starlet, the full text of the Surrender document signed by the Germans, and an editorial that warned that Russia was becoming the number one problem for Americans. Oh, and there were photographs of young Americans that might have been taken at a concentration camp. Though they were smiling at the camera they were gaunt, with their ribs sticking out, all bone and flesh with no fat.

The four-page photo spread in the July 30, 1945 issue, had the heading "Men Starve in Minnesota." It showed 36 volunteers who had voluntarily signed up to be starved nearly to death in order to teach scientists the effects of hunger and strategies for restoring starving people. These individuals were conscientious objectors who had been filtered through a rigorous screening program before being accepted. They were mostly Mennonites, Quakers, and Brethren who, because of their understanding of the words of Jesus in the Sermon on the Mount and their church's stance against war, could not take another person's life. However, all were already serving their nation in alternative service. They were anxious to demonstrate that they were as willing to take risks as those in the front line. Also, they were idealistic and looking for a way to help humanity through their service to the nation.

The rules were strict. The men were given jobs to perform and were expected to be very active, even as they received fewer and fewer calories every day. In addition to their time on the treadmill they were required to walk 22 miles outdoors, every week, regardless of the weather. Minnesota winters could be cruel.

Participants discovered that they no longer cared about literature, sports, music, and most especially women. These healthy young men lost interest in everything but food. They eagerly consumed every scrap that was given them, licking their plates clean. Their body weight dropped dramatically until they were literally skin and bones.

The program was not designed by a mad scientist, but a respected researcher who wanted to learn more about the physiology of starvation to better help those who would be rehabilitating the population of Europe when the war ended. Dr. Ancel Keys had established his reputation in medicine and nutrition with his invention of the K Ration, which provided a healthy balanced diet to soldiers in the field. Following the war, he was the researcher who established the link between diet, cholesterol, and heart disease. The massive two-volume study that resulted from the Starvation Experiment, *The Biology of Human Starvation*, is the only sanctioned study of its kind. It would no longer be ethical to produce such a study, and it has proven priceless not only for the rehabilitation of starving people, but also has provided data essential to the study of eating disorders such as anorexia.

Meanwhile, the participants were gradually restored to full health. They went on to live normal lives after the war and recovered from the experiment without any long-term health problems. They continued to serve in their churches, satisfied they had shown that the way of peace is also the way of service in the name of Jesus.

Jesus taught his apostles the way of peace, but as he said in the gospel of John, "Peace I give, not as the world gives...." The conscientious objectors believed that following the way of peace in the name of Jesus meant to be even more actively engaged in the world than before.

Ascension of Our Lord
Ephesians 1:15-23
by David O. Bales

The Eyes of the Heart Enlightened

"Why did you sleep?" the man of the family asked the boy. "All the villagers' cattle could stray — and our cow among them." He glared at the boy, who didn't answer. "These babies need milk. We took you in and gave you milk as a child. You pay us back by endangering all cows of the village."

When the boy was caught that first time he was sentenced to weeding the garden with the girls for a week — a terrible dishonor. He would never again lie down to sleep while herding the cattle. But he found a position to sit where he could sleep and appear to be alert. By sitting on something higher than the bare ground and drooping his head to his chest, from a distance his napping passed undetected. If he were to sleep any other way, an adult from the village or another shepherd would discover him and tell his family.

The boy stood now and stretched after a few heartbeats of very warm sleep. He counted the cattle through the distortion of the desert air. Nine, ten, eleven… one wandered toward the brush. The boy set out in a steady jog to circle it and haze it back. Eleven cows, one for each family. Here on the edge of the Ethiopian desert, few villages were larger. The boy knew two other villages: one was three days east into the desert, the other two days west into the striped hills.

As he ran to chase back the cow he thought about the banter in the village. Everyone was talking about them. They would come from the sky and then walk to the village. If only children spoke of such, he could disregard the news — but even the adults he lived with agreed. For twelve days the village spoke of their coming more than it complained of the extreme heat. They're coming tomorrow.

The boy shooed and switched the cattle farther for their afternoon grazing. Fortunately, here he could sit in the partial shade of a bush. He liked to get a little shade every day, especially now in the oppressive heat; but the cows always moved farther than he wanted them. If he stood right beside them, they still insisted on one step farther.

They never stayed where he led. He, however... he must follow his precise orders every day. No step further of freedom for him. Someone told him the direction and distance. The cattle had more choice than he did and when he brought the cattle home at night, people were glad only to see their cow.

He'd herded cows since his sixth summer. During his eleventh summer he was doing the same thing and living in the same borrowed home. Nothing changed. Certainly nothing got better. One thing was different today — because the desert had received one of its rare rainfalls, the boy found a puddle a handwidth across that the cows hadn't spied. He looked into its muddy water and saw the outline of his head and shoulders. Three, perhaps four years ago he'd seen his outline in a puddle. He didn't remember his head seeming as large. He could ask the woman in the family if he'd grown much in three years, but she'd probably do as usual when he talked: sigh, turn away, and begin to scrape out a pot or make bread.

The next day the boy again took the cattle where he was told. Again he sat and pretended to watch them. He closed his eyes. They'll arrive today. They've left their giant village and entered a room that flies. They're coming to teach about Jesus. The boy gladly anticipated their arrival. When the village gathered to dance and sing he felt less alone.

By the time the boy drove the cattle to the village that evening, groups of people were gathered on the field next to the village. He left each cow at its hut, then strode quickly toward a loud group of children crowded around two light-skinned men. One man stepped forward to a girl and the interpreter pointed to the light-skinned man, "Look at him. Look." Soon they bent down together to look at something the boy couldn't see and the children around screamed, "You. You. That's you." The girl laughed, trying to stop her giggling with both hands, scuffing her feet and stirring up puffs of dust. The next child said, "Me! Me!"

The boy didn't know what caused the uproar in the center of the crowd. He stood on tiptoes at the edge of the group. The lighter-skinned men wore hats with bills in front and shirts with long sleeves clinging with sweat. One light-skinned man looked over the other children to him and said something. The boy didn't understand. The light-faced man gestured with a cupped hand. The interpreter said to the boy, "Come. Come." The other children moved to let him by. A light-faced man raised the small, shiny box near his face and seemed to aim at the boy. The boy heard a click. The man turned the box around and held it down to the boy. "Look," the interpreter said. "Look here."

The boy looked at a tiny picture of a boy's face. He didn't know why the man was holding it to him or who the boy was in this vividly clear picture. He cocked his head to the side like a confused dog. The girl beside him laughed and screamed with delight, "That's you, Lema. That's you, Lema."

Lema looked at the girl beside him who was saying his name. Then Lema looked at the interpreter holding the shiny picture box. The man said, "Lema?" He pointed to the picture. "Lema, that's you. God made you, Lema, and Jesus knows your name and what you look like. And Jesus loves *you*, Lema, as though you were the only person in the world to love."

Easter 7
John 17:20-26
by Stan Purdum

In All His Glory

Father, I desire that those also, whom you have given me, may be with me where I am, to see my glory, which you have given me because you loved me before the foundation of the world.
— John 17:24

When Brittany and her seven-year-old son Brandon arrived at the play area in the park on Thursday, Jenny was already there. Thursdays were her day to watch her grandson Mark, who was also seven. As soon as the two boys were turned loose on the playground, they applied themselves vigorously to the monkey bars and swings. Jenny was already seated on a nearby park bench, and Brittany sank down wearily beside her. Despite their age difference, the two women had become friends since meeting in the park.

"Hi Brittany," Jenny said. "You look worn out."

"Oh, I am. It's getting to be such a battle with Brandon every time we go anywhere to get him to dress properly for the weather. I mean, it can't be more than 55 degrees today, but he refuses to wear a hat. He says nobody wears them at school. So there he is, hatless. You must think I'm a bad mother."

Jenny chuckled. "Not at all. Haven't you heard that old saying that 'A sweater is an item a child has to put on when his mother feels cold'?"

"That's cute, but..."

"Listen, Brittany, there must be a difference in metabolism between children and their parents. I don't know if any scientific evidence exists to verify it, but kids seem to run hotter than grown-ups. You should have seen me when

Mark's father was born. He was our first child, and I was determined to be a good mother. The first time I took him outside, I dressed him in a sleeper, a sweater, a coat, and a hat with ear flaps, and then I wrapped him in a quilted blanket."

"What's wrong with that?" Brittany asked.

"It was *July*."

Both women laughed.

"I guess I do need to lighten up a bit," Brittany said.

"Oh, you'll learn soon enough. Kids have a way of teaching us. Brandon's resisting the hat now, but wait a bit. Pretty soon he won't want to wear any of the clothes you've so lovingly selected for him. At school, what the other kids are wearing has a huge influence."

"Actually, that's already started."

"Have you gotten to the 'at least' stage yet?" Jenny asked.

"What's that?"

"It's what parents say after they realize that the dressing-the-kid battle is lost. As in 'Well, if you don't want to wear your raincoat, at least take an umbrella,' or 'If you won't wear that warm hat I bought for you, at least put on a scarf.' And then there's 'All right, you don't have to wear your mittens, but at least take them with you in your book bag.'"

"That's what's ahead? Good grief."

"The people who live next door to me have a twelve-year-old. He wears short pants every month of the year. I know his mother makes him 'at least' put on a warm jacket in cold months. I know this because he regularly leaves it behind at my house when he goes home without it after playing with Brian — that's Mark's older brother. He often comes to our house after school."

Brittany laughed despite her frustration.

Jenny continued, "The other losing battle is getting kids to dress appropriately for whatever occasion is at hand —

such as going to church. Brian and Mark's mom told me about a dust-up they had last Sunday morning when they were getting ready to go to church. She had Mark attired in dress pants and a nice sweater. But then Brian came out of his room in jeans and a T-shirt. Naturally, she told him to change, and naturally he resisted. She stood her ground, but when Brian returned, he had put on clothes only marginally better. And by that time they were running late, so they went with that. But then Mark started in with, 'If Brian gets to wear jeans, why can't I?' And it went downhill from there."

"It sounds daunting," Brittany observed.

"Well, it is, I suppose. But after a while you learn to pick your battles. Sometimes the clothes thing just isn't that important. But you do have one line of defense, you know."

"I do? Tell me."

"Kids don't do their own laundry. You do. And when they get attached to certain garments you really don't like, you have the ability to make them 'magically' disappear in the wash."

"I'll remember that," Brittany said. "Now, if we could only figure a way to make hats and mittens 'magically' appear on their heads and hands."

***

In John 17:24, Jesus prays that his followers may see his glory. Sometimes we miss his glory because we try to dress him in garments of our choosing. We dress him as the sweet, permissive savior or the enlightened sage or the "man's man" or the gentle shepherd or the super social worker or as some other favorite image. But we need to stand back and view the full image of Jesus from the scriptures. When we do, his glory will be apparent.

About the Authors

David O. Bales was a Presbyterian (USA) pastor for 33 years, and is a graduate of the University of Portland (where he was editor of the yearbook) and San Francisco Theological Seminary. In addition to his ministry, he also has taught college: World Religions, Ethics, Biblical Hebrew and Biblical Greek (recently at College of Idaho). He has been a freelance researcher, writer, and editor for Stephen Ministries. His sermons and articles have appeared in *Interpretation*, *Pulpit Digest*, *Preaching*, *Lectionary Homiletics*, *Emphasis*, and *Preaching the Great Texts*. He wrote a year-long online column: "In The Original: Insights from Greek and Hebrew for the Lectionary Passages." His books include: *Gospel Subplots: Story Sermons of God's Grace*; *Toward Easter and Beyond*; *Scenes of Glory: Subplots of God's Long Story*; and *To the Cross and Beyond: Cycle A Sermons for Lent and Easter*, all available at CSS Publishing Company.

Scott Dalgarno is pastor of Wasatch Presbyterian Church in Salt Lake City, Utah. Born in California, he has previously served four Presbyterian churches in Oregon. He is a graduate of Whitworth University, University of Oregon, and San Francisco Theological Seminary. A poet, his poems have appeared in *The Christian Century*, *America*, *The Antioch Review*, and *Yale Review*.

Sandra Herrmann is a retired pastor and popular teacher in the Wisconsin Conference of the United Methodist Church. She is a poet and the author of *Ambassadors of Hope* (CSS). She has been published in *alive now!*, a magazine of spirituality of the UMC, *Emphasis* magazine for pastors, and currently writes monthly for *StoryShare*. She is working on a book exploring the Christian iconography of the Harry Potter series.

Keith Hewitt is the author of two volumes of *NaTiVity Dramas: Nontraditional Christmas Plays for All Ages* (CSS). He is a local pastor, co-youth leader, an occasional speaker at Christmas events, and former Sunday school teacher at Wilmot United Methodist Church in Wilmot, Wisconsin. He lives in southeastern Wisconsin with his wife, two children, and assorted dogs and cats.

Craig Kelly received his B.A. from the University of Saskatchewan in 2002. He and his wife, Beth, are actively involved in their church, working both in their church's children's ministry as well as working with low-income youth in their neighborhood. Craig enjoys reading, music, hiking, biking, and indulging in old sci-fi movies.

C. David McKirachan is pastor of the Presbyterian Church at Shrewsbury in central New Jersey. He also teaches at Monmouth University. McKirachan is the author of *I Happened Upon a Miracle* and *A Year of Wonder* (Westminster John Knox).

Rick McCracken-Bennett is an Episcopal priest, storyteller, writer, musician, and church planter. He is a member of the Storytellers of Central Ohio and the National Storytelling Network. His doctoral dissertation concerned the use of story to guide congregations into the future that God intends for them. He is the rector of All Saints Episcopal Church in New Albany, Ohio, where a sermon wouldn't be a sermon without a good story.

Stan Purdum, a United Methodist minister, is a freelance writer and editor. His books include *He Walked in Galilee*, about the ministry of Jesus (Abingdon Press, 2005) and *New Mercies I See*, short stories about God's grace (CSS Publishing Company, Inc., 2003), as well as four books about bicycling. He has been published in religious and secular journals, has authored numerous sermons for lectionary volumes and preaching journals, and writes adult Sunday school curriculum. Stan and his wife, Jeanine, live in North Canton, Ohio. They have three grown children.

Frank Ramirez has served as a pastor for nearly 30 years in Church of the Brethren congregations in Los Angeles, California; Elkhart, Indiana; and Everett, Pennsylvania. A graduate of LaVerne College and Bethany Theological Seminary, Ramirez is the author of numerous books, articles, and short stories. His CSS titles include *Partners in Healing*, *He Took a Towel*, *The Bee Attitudes*, and three volumes of *Lectionary Worship Aids*.

Argile Smith is Vice President for Advancement at William Carey University in Hattiesburg, Mississippi. He previously served at New Orleans Baptist Theological Seminary (NOBTS) as a preaching professor, chairman of the Division of Pastoral Ministries, and director of the communications center. While at NOTBS, Smith regularly hosted the Gateway to Truth program on the FamilyNet television network. He has also been the pastor of several congregations in Louisiana and Mississippi. Smith's articles have been widely published in church periodicals, and he is the author or editor of four books.

Peter Andrew Smith is an ordained minister in the United Church of Canada, currently serving St. James United Church in Antigonish, Nova Scotia. He is the author of *All Things Are Ready* (CSS), a book of lectionary-based communion prayers. He is also the author of a number of stories and articles, which can be found listed at www.peterandrewsmith.com.

The Rt. Rev. John S. Smylie, Bishop of Wyoming, previously served as the rector of St. Mark's Episcopal Church in Casper, Wyoming, and as the dean of the Cathedral of St. John the Evangelist in Spokane, Washington. He is a published author and storyteller as well as a singer-songwriter. Smylie recently completed *Grace for Today*, a collection of 25 stories that explores how grace, loss, and restoration are part of the same fabric.

John Sumwalt is the pastor of Our Lord's United Methodist Church in New Berlin, Wisconsin, and a noted storyteller. He is the author of nine books, including the acclaimed *Vision Stories* series and *How to Preach the Miracles: Why People Don't Believe Them and What You Can Do About It*. John and his wife Jo Perry-Sumwalt served for three years as the co-editors of *StoryShare*. A graduate of the University of Wisconsin-Madison and the University of Dubuque Theological Seminary (UDTS), Sumwalt received the Herbert Manning Jr. award for parish ministry from UDTS in 1997.

Larry Winebrenner graduated from Garrett Biblical Institute (now Garrett Evangelical Theological Seminary) over fifty years ago. He has been published in such varied publications as *The Christian Advocate*, *Games* magazine, and *Numismatic News*. He has been a contributor to *StoryShare* for a number of years. Larry served churches in Georgia, the Florida Keys, Indiana, and Wisconsin before returning to Miami, Florida, to teach at Miami-Dade College. He was an essential part of seeing the institution grow from a few classes held in a converted chicken coop to becoming the largest college in the United States of America. He now holds the title of Professor Emeritus from that institution.

www.ingramcontent.com/pod-product-compliance
Lightning Source LLC
Chambersburg PA
CBHW071756040426
42446CB00012B/2579